BUILDING STRONGER

BROTHERS
&
SISTERS

BY: Michael Muse

All rights reserved by Michael Muse. This book or any portion thereof may not be reproduced or used in any manner whatsoever without the expressed written permission of the publisher except the use of brief quotations in a book review.

ISBN: 979-8-218-13972-8

Cover designed by Driven by Design Creative Agency LLC
All rights owned and reserved by Michael Muse

ABOUT THE AUTHOR

Michael Muse is a New Jersey native, born July 16, 1986. Michael is the oldest of two from mother Pamela Muse and father Michael Muse.

In 2009, Michael graduated Summa Cum Laude with a bachelor's degree in business administration from the oldest historically black institution of knowledge, Cheyney University. There he was a member of the collegiate football team, as well as the track and field team, where he was recognized for multiple school and conference achievements. He also became a member of Omega Psi Phi Fraternity Inc. in the spring of 2007. While serving within the fraternity during his tenure as an undergraduate, Michael received the Fraternity's highest academic award, International Scholar of the Year (2008).

Shortly after graduation Michael enlisted within the United States Army and quickly thereafter completed Officer Candidate School to become a Commissioned Officer. As a commissioned officer Michael deployed and managed a team in Afghanistan from 2013-2014.

Less than 3 months after his return from Afghanistan, Michael attended North Carolina Agricultural and Technical State University where he obtained his master's degree in Business Administration with a concentration in Supply Chain Systems.

Upon completion of his MBA in 2016, Michael focused on becoming a well-rounded individual in his craft by performing in various positions within one of the largest oil companies in the world, as well as the military simultaneously. Michael still currently serves in the United States Army full-time.

DEDICATIONS

To my parents whose sacrifices created the foundation, to which I started my journey.

To my aunts whose achievements motivated me to create my blueprint and remain persistent despite all obstacles that I have faced along the way.

To my friends and loved ones who showed me that thriving is possible.

To the brave brilliant youth who are entering the unknown. Stay true to your plan and never lose sight of your goals.

The baton has been passed and I am to carry this leg of the marathon in a race we all call life. I am not the leading leg, nor am I the anchor. When I pass the baton, we shall be in a better position than when we started. I am focused, determined, and vow to execute. Not a misstep, nor a glance backwards, we shall forever move forward. Losing is not an option.

- Michael Muse

TABLE OF CONTENTS

Introduction	14
Wake Up Call	22
It Starts Here	26
Parent Conversations	32
What Are You Going to Do?	36
Building the Foundation	40
Second Time Around	48
Building A Network	54
Civilian Vs. Military Transition	62
Mentors Vs. Role Models	66
Never Get Time Back	78
Time to Make Moves	82
Conclusion	90
Let's Connect	94

"Not only am I literally and figuratively the dark horse, I'm actually the poor horse. The only thing that I have going for me is my soul and my commitment to the American People."

- Shirley Chisholm

INTRODUCTION

In my life, I have had many achievements. I graduated Summa Cum Laude with a bachelor's in business administration. I joined a world-renowned Fraternity and earned several of their highest academic awards. I also enlisted in the United States Army and later became a Commissioned Officer. I served overseas in Afghanistan, where I had the honor of managing and leading soldiers within a combat zone. I furthered my education and obtained my MBA with a concentration in Supply Chain Systems. I also participated in a Leadership program in the largest oil company in the world; and I now continue to lead and contribute to the development of Soldiers at all levels of the US Army on a full-time basis.

When you see those things, you think you did all this because you had help. How can I achieve those things, you don't have to deal with the things I deal with? Nobody is going to give me the chance to do those things. What if I told you I gave that brief overview, just to say that with all these accomplishments; growing up, I had no idea what I wanted to do with my life. I didn't even know what kind of jobs and businesses existed outside of the local factories and warehouses in the area. In fact, the majority of my jobs were given to me through temp agencies growing up. I didn't even really care about school; I was going to school because I liked playing sports. I also knew that to play sports I had to maintain my grades; otherwise, I wouldn't have done the work, despite how easy I perceived the work to be. When I wasn't in school, I was just out roaming and having fun. My scope and outlook on life went no further than the city limits. I figured when I'm done with school I'm going to work in a factory or just go to the military. I was following down the path of someone destined to be nothing more than a statistic soon to be overlooked by society. It would have been easy to carry out that narrative; because society was programming me to accept that scenario. I was unknowingly being conditioned to follow suit and take what society deemed was my predetermined place in life. However, after receiving a second chance on life after an unfortunate event, I just knew I was meant to do more. I didn't know what that more was, but I wanted to figure it out.

A community is a collection of people in a specific location. Each community is made up of many sub-systems which consists of people performing various tasks which contribute to the overall flow of that system. Either by design or by coincidence everyone within that system has a key task essential to the success of that system. When that individual performing that key task within that system is gone; someone else will fill that void and the system will continue. Not all positions are glorified. Some people find themselves in positions that are less ideal, because of a series of decisions and unfortunate experiences. On the other hand, some people will learn through a series of experiences and achieve great things throughout their lifetime. Inadvertently, either consciously or subconsciously due to the norms of society, people are being groomed at an early age to take over the reins and eventually become those same people they observed growing up.

Growing up, everyone at some point has heard their parents or an adult tell them "I want you to do better than me"; "you can do anything"; or the token phrase "get you a degree and get a good job". All of these statements are true, and most adults in your life genuinely want you to do better than them; but they can't guide you there. The reality is people can only prepare you to get to their level. Even though, their intentions are pure; they just don't know all the factors that contribute to reaching that next state because they haven't been there. They are imagining what it would be like, just like you.

For some individuals, they don't have parents or guardians to look to for guidance. They learn through experience, which is dictated by their environment. To add to that, most people aren't even aware of just how different life is beyond where they live. This contributes to views and goals that are limited to what they have observed. It's not their fault; people at all ages are just consumed with maneuvering through day-to-day scenarios that they don't even have time to think about the possibilities outside their current experience. As a result, some find themselves in a routine which keeps them constricted to where they are.

On the other hand, some children are fortunate enough to grow up in more stable environments, places where they are able to bear witness to success. Their parents are in better situations than most, educated and career driven; their foundation is set on effective routines they observed while growing up. While they are growing up, due to the successful mindsets of their Parents and people around them, they will receive mentorship geared towards obtaining success like their parents and the adults in their life. As long as they are open to receiving that mentorship; they will follow in the footsteps of the ones before them. Simply because they have been shown what to do, why they are doing it, and what impact these actions will have on their future.

Some individuals coming from adverse situations that make the right decisions and avoid the distractions of their environment will receive opportunities to move on and do great things. The individuals from the more fortunate situations will move on to do great things, as well. The difference, one will be groomed and will already possess the tools and confidence necessary to succeed. The other will be entering a whole new world where everything will be foreign to them. It will be up to them to adapt and overcome in an expeditious fashion.

The biggest thing that sets most young individuals apart is what they experience during their upbringing. No one is smarter than the other, no one has the inability to learn. The only difference is the mentorship, education, and exposure these individuals have received up to that point. Individuals who come from backgrounds that are different than their current situation must enter opportunities with the mentality that they are a bag of raw talent that must position themselves in a way to receive the guidance necessary to succeed in their new environment. With the right guidance, combined with their work ethic and enthusiasm, they will be successful at anything they are taught to do.

Unfortunately, not all companies promote growth or have the time and patience to train personnel on an individual basis. Not when the market has so many experienced individuals to choose from. They only care about whether this individual can deliver in the role they have been selected for. Some people are fortunate enough to obtain mentors once they enter the workforce, which is good; but how often do people, especially just entering the work scene, even know the significance of finding a mentor that is fully vested in your success? Until a new employee discovers an effective mentor everything must be self-driven.

Sad to say these situations occur early and often for some; and the further you progress than the people around you, the less guidance they can provide you along the way. Even if their intentions are good, realistically, a person can't guide you effectively through scenarios that they haven't experienced firsthand. In other words, a person can only get you as far as they have gone themselves.

It is that grooming at a young age which develops you and prepares you for all the experiences you shall have in your life. How many first generational people can say they actually had someone sitting them down and walking through the proper procedures and how to maneuver certain situations that will allow them to progress professionally? Not many, this means that at some point every situation they encounter are first time experiences and depending on what decisions they make in those situations; they could find themselves right back to square one. That is a lot of Pressure!

This is the reason I wrote this. This book is for people seeking to go to the next level in their life; but don't feel they have anyone around who could provide the proper guidance needed. Like I touched on earlier; people can only prepare you to get to their level. I am a young professional that has overcome many challenges and have managed to find success along the way. I have experience in both the private and government sector. While displaying the ability to exceed the standards set before me; I also, acknowledge that I had a lot of unnecessary struggles along the way. Many of my hardships were simply because I was not prepared due to lack of experience and awareness. I don't regret any of the experiences that I had because it made me who I am today. However, as enriching as those experiences were, I feel that it is essential that I share the things I have learned with those who desire to be prepared, as opposed to trial by fire. Not everyone has to learn the hard way.

The book will be laid out in phases starting with high school and ending in the career phase (I can only teach you to reach my level). Your foundation starts in high school as far as being a future contributor to society is concerned. For this reason, we will begin there. Following that the book will then enter the college years. This is where you are preparing yourself to do what you ultimately want to do in life. From there we transition into entry-level positions; this is where you determine the environment you desire to work in. Lastly, we position ourselves to follow a specific career path.

Depending on where you are in life; or if you have a loved one who is pursuing a path that you are not familiar with, this book should be able to assist in steering you or them in the right direction.

"To know how much there is to know is the beginning of learning to live"

- Dorothy West

WAKE UP CALL

I grew up in NJ born in the north and raised in the south. I had both of my parents growing up. My father was a Marine who later transferred into the Air Force Reserves and became a full-time Postal Worker. My mother had a career working her way up at a bank. They were hardworking folks, not rich but survivors who were able to find their lane and provide the most stable lives possible for me and my sister, given our surroundings. Neither of them went to college, but growing up they were always saying things like, "go to college and get a good job"; "find a job and work real hard and retire". Aside from this narrative that was being programmed into me, I never really had a lot of people teaching me what to do. There is a goal or intent; and there is the procedures or plan to achieve the goal. A lot of people always talk to me about goals, but never had conversations on how to go about achieving those goals. In fact, I took a lot of my lessons from learning what not to do. What I mean by that is, I would just observe the mental state of everyone around me and how they appeared in or after different situations. If they didn't appear happy or at least content, I would avoid dealing with those similar situations. Except for brief moments, most of the people around me just didn't appear happy most of the time. I analyze their current state and reflect on their activities I've observed and from that I would make a decision on whether or not I would do things similar. I didn't know what to do, but I knew I wasn't going to do what they were doing.

In NJ depending on where you live, it is a labor-based society which consists of mostly factory and warehouse work. If you could become a tractor trailer driver, law enforcement or get a job working for public transportation, then in our eyes you made it. Some people joined the armed forces and left the area altogether (which majority of my family did). Essentially, the goal was to graduate high school then move out on your own and do what needs to be done. From the time you graduate high school, you have to figure it out and just make do with what you have. Most of us, coming out of high school, have nothing. So essentially, we start behind.

I paint that picture to better explain, fast-forwarding to when I graduated from college and got a decent job (at least in my mind because I was getting paid more than I ever did in my life). I found myself in the DMV area (Washington DC – Maryland-Virginia area). Through my fraternity, I was able to meet and form friendships with like-minded individuals from colleges all over the United States that relocated and have already become familiar with the area. Coming from NJ after just graduating from a small HBCU (Cheyney University, the first HBCU); in my eyes, these people were living the dream. Going on group trips, fancy restaurants, nice cars, and nice houses. Up to that point, I had never seen individuals living like them in real life; especially at our age. Everything they were introducing to me was a culture shock; and I liked it. I was not where they were in life, but I was motivated to get there. In addition to just lifestyle, they were just aware of everyday business moves, just the terms alone were foreign to me. It was apparent to me that I was behind the curve. As time went on, I realized none of us were any smarter than the others; so being underqualified was not the case. I was just simply unaware of the opportunities that existed outside of my previous environment; this was a result of my lack of exposure (you only know what you were taught or experience). I wanted to learn what they were doing to actually obtain those levels of success. A lot of successful people say you want to center
yourself around people who are doing more than you are. These people were that for me; this group showed me that, not only is there so much out there I was yet to tap in to; but I also had the ability to obtain it. This ignited a spark in me; the goal now was to thrive, not just survive.

"Be passionate and move forward with gusto every single hour of every single day until you reach your goal"

- Ava Duvernay

IT STARTS HERE

We start here in high school, because of the significance of this time frame. By high school, you are operating off the core values that have been programed into you by your parents up to this point. You are also operating in a space where you have less supervision and the ones who raised you are under the impression that you have the ability to execute what you have been taught. High school is your chance to demonstrate that you are able to execute freely, while still in a controlled environment. Also, you begin to operate under the premise of what you believe is correct, which may or may not be contradictory to what your guardians have taught you. The reason is your mind has been shaped by a combination of your guardians, school, peers and your environment. You are now a freethinker, but there is still some monitoring to mitigate the ramifications of your actions (whether you believe it or not, you are not an adult yet). As a freethinker, you are able to determine what drives you. You begin to find more hobbies; you start to notice your strengths and weaknesses; as well as significant things that set you apart from everyone else. Some of these things can be academics, sports, hobbies, and just life experiences in general. In addition, high school is where you start to get recognized for those talents and abilities. The most important thing during this time is building upon those newly acquired skills.

High school is the place where you start to get an idea of what you are good at, as well as ultimately what you want to do with your life (some discover it earlier than others). High school provides you with the resources and or environment to begin developing those skills (some places have more resources than others). It also gives you the opportunity to see where you are in comparison to others doing things similar to you. You can learn where your performance gaps are and what others do to improve themselves and you can implement those tactics, as well. But the ultimate purpose for high school is to develop the blueprint for what you are going to do with the rest of your life. Sometimes what you want to do and what you are good at don't always coincide. This is what makes developing a blueprint so important. You can be good at something, but not want to do it for the rest of your life. So, understanding where you realistically are in comparison to others doing what you want to do is important, because your journey may be longer or more difficult than others.

While in high school, once you get an idea of what you want to do with your life the planning begins. Whether it be a trade, instrument or sports related you now have your intent. With that intent your thought process must now move towards "what do I have to do to obtain that goal". There are certain criteria you must meet in order to be considered an individual that does what you want to do well. In order to meet that criteria, you must obtain and develop the skills that relate to that specific trade. How do you develop those skills? By positioning yourself in a place that is recognized for developing those skills and learn as much out of that location that you can. Rather it be a trade school, University, or mentor (depending on what you are actually doing). You must research what schools are known for what you want to do and work towards attending those schools. Growing up everyone is putting so much pressure on you to go to college; that people just go to any college just for the sake of going to college. Another thing people do is choose colleges based on all the hype that revolves around a school. Your choice in colleges should never be based on how fun the campus looks or can be. Your purpose for going to school is to prepare you to get a job in a specific field, fun in college is inevitable. You must look at the schools that provide the best resources to develop the skills necessary for what you ultimately want to do. School, whether it be a trade school or university, should be looked at as the steppingstone to the next level of your life and not just something to do.

Aside from resources, when schools are known for developing quality people in specific fields, they are already on successful companies' radar. Sports is not the only career where recruiters come out to search for the next great one. Aside from job fairs, recruiters do come to schools known for specific skills looking to hire people for jobs, the more your school is known for a program and or skill the more recruiters come seeking people who are showing great potential in that field. Therefore, it is important to know what the schools you are looking to go to are known for and why. Businesses aren't going to med schools looking for accountants; just like Hospitals aren't going to law schools looking for doctors. You can be great at something, but if you are not positioned in the right place; being recognized becomes more difficult.

Another thing that makes choosing the right school for building your foundation, is the resources a school invests into a department. In a perfect world a school should divide the funds and resources evenly; however, in reality the most successful departments in a school get the majority of the funding. Just going to a school for the sake of going to school could find you in a position where you have so much potential, but opportunities aren't coming your way because the school is not known for the field you are pursuing. As a result, programs and jobs to further develop outside of school will not be communicated to you. Yes, you could do research on your own; but you are not going to find everything, and you have to know where to look. There could be opportunities out there pertaining to your chosen skillset that you could be unaware of simply because you are not in a place to receive the information.

If college or a trade do not fall in line with things that you want to do, you can always consider the military. Yeah, I know in some places it gets a bad rap; but the military has a lot to offer. This is ideal for people who don't know what they want to do (not everyone knows what they want to do right out of high school) but know that they are going to be on their own very soon (because in some families, unfortunately when you turn 18 you are getting out the house prepared or not). The military gives you an opportunity to perform unique jobs that you can't get trained for in college. Depending on what you do while in the military you can obtain well-paying jobs outside of the military that individuals with degrees don't even qualify for. So even if you don't commit to a full 20+ year career in the military; it is a great place to start and build upon your foundation until you figure it out. You can start making money right out of school and get an opportunity to live somewhere new. I highly recommend individuals move after high school to experience different cultures; this will help you become more diverse and assist with dealing with people from different backgrounds and further develop your foundation. I can honestly say, in my experience, a lot of doors opened for me after I joined the Army. I'm not sure if it was from my new outlook on life or the experience I gained; but I received more opportunities than I could ever imagine (I was also not aware of all the opportunities that were out there until after I joined, as well) and I owe a great deal of gratitude to the US Army.

Not everyone wants to go to college, I understand that. You don't have to go to college to be successful, but you must be realistic about what type of salary an individual in your career field makes. Society has utilized numerous platforms to convince the masses that anybody can be a millionaire for doing just about anything; this could not be further from the truth. Understanding this will avoid a lot of disappointment and resentment in the future. Importantly, it will prevent a lot of unnecessary effort, energy and time. You must be as intentional as possible when working towards a goal; everything you do is either working towards, away, or delaying that goal. If you realize along the way that you want to do something else that is ok, but you must understand; the process begins when you commit to a plan. No matter what you try to do **BE INTENTIONAL.**

"It is easier to build strong children than to repair broken men"

- Frederick Douglass

PARENT CONVERSATIONS

Often at times, parents are too consumed with working and providing for their children to have conversations revolving around college and their future plans. Also, if they didn't go to college, where would they start the conversation? They can encourage the children to apply to colleges, but how much knowledge will they have of the colleges their children are applying to? Usually, people who grow up in households where their parents or guardians didn't go to college, aren't discussing college at all. Most conversations are merely the adults around them asking, so what are you going to do? You are going to be an adult soon. It's time to make grown decisions, but throughout time, they have not been conditioning them to make those decisions. The adults in your life are just so happy that you got into college, they are not concerned with what degree you are pursuing or even what college you are going to. They are going out on faith that you will come out of college and get a good job.

Below are some important questions that I feel should be brought to the attention of children in relation to furthering their education beyond high school:

What are you trying to be when you get older?

What is your plan to do that?

Have you thought about a school?

What type of school are you thinking about going to?

Have you made a list of schools that you want to apply to?

Why did you choose these schools?

(If possible) Let's schedule a visit?

As parents/ guardians, it is up to you to do research, as well. You should view the schools and confirm if they fall in line with the child's plan. Also, through numerous conversations you can get a better idea of what the mind state of the child is and confirm that the child is really taking the decision process seriously or is at least heading in the right direction. Depending on responses, you may have to redirect the child and get them on track before they go too far to the left.

"Have a vision of excellence, a dream of success, and work like hell"

- Dr. Samuel DuBois Cook

WHAT ARE YOU GOING TO DO?

At an early age my parents always harped on the importance of school. "Get good grades, go to college, get one of them business degrees and get a good job," they would always say. Luckily for me, regardless of what I did or how I acted, I always got good grades. In spite of their teachings, neither of them went to college. They were hard working folks that did the best they could with what they had. Now that I'm older, I realized they were simply feeding me what society fed to them; all with good intentions of course. Through their experience they viewed getting a degree as the key to a better life (rightfully so) and were dead set on making sure I and my sister believed in that philosophy, as well.

Growing up you are taught the natural order of life was you graduate high school, go to college, graduate, and get a good job. Everything was pushing that same message (family, television, books, etc.); I'm going to be telling my age here, but we use to have television shows for kids, called after school specials and occasionally, they had those episodes talking about college. I was programmed into believing my goal was to follow that vision, which during that time seemed like the most well thought out plan to life. But that was the problem, that vision was my plan; just as detailed as it is stated above. My plan was an overview. Besides the overview of going to college, getting a business degree and getting a good job, which my parents harped on all the time, they never really sat me down and walked through what those steps really looked like. As time grew closer for me to graduate my parents and family kept harping on "go to college and get a good job". We never discussed potential colleges, what I wanted do (I didn't know anyways), never looked at applications and the only college visit I did was when my friend's parents took us up to a college to visit (neither of us went to that college, might I add). I applied to one college on a bad computer and wasn't aware that my application was completely blank when I submitted it (I didn't go to that college either).

Fortunately, for me I always had good grades; so somehow NJ made a decision that last semester of my senior year, that if you are within the top 20% of your graduating class you can go to community college in your county for free. I applied to community college and got accepted. Great, I'm going to college, and getting a business degree, I am about to get a good job! The plot thickens a little later, but I was full of hope for the time being.

With that said, education is important, regardless of what type of school you choose to attend. Do your best and put forth an effort to get the best grades you can. More opportunities are available when you have good grades than when you don't. Not saying that not having good grades stops you, but it'd be better to have and not need than need and not have (this carries over to a lot of things in life). Even while not getting into a big-time university (barely applied to any), I still had an opportunity to do something as a result of the grades I had.

"You can only become accomplished at something you love. Don't make money your goal. Instead pursue the things you love doing and then do them so well that people can't take their eyes off you."

- Maya Angelou

BUILDING THE FOUNDATION

After all of the research, requests and deliberation amongst what the next steps are for your life; you have found a higher institution of education that is willing to facilitate your pursuit of a career. Congratulations!! No matter what type of school you are attending, you must understand this; this is a crucial period in your life. This is the point where you must assess your new environment and determine what resources, in that given space, will be utilized to create the foundation that you will be building on for the rest of your life. There is no one around to keep you on track or to push you. Your future is now in your hands. Don't be the one to get so consumed into this new level of freedom that you lose track of what you really came to school to do. To obtain a career in a chosen field. This is where the discipline and understanding comes into play. Your thought process now must transition to, how does what I'm doing get me closer to obtaining the career/ life I want. Also, because we are manifesting; how does this prepare me to perform when I get the job that I want. Everything you do from this moment forward must be looked at as an investment into your future. You are either getting closer to your goal or further away.

In both trade school and college, you are there to develop a skillset that you will utilize to generate income for the rest of your life. With that being said, if this is something that upon completion you are claiming that you can do; wouldn't you want to be as good at it as you possibly can? Fortunately, the school you attend (if you have utilized the planning methods in the previous chapter) will have additional resources to develop your skill set beyond the classroom. It is now up to you to seek them out. These resources could be in the form of clubs, labs, or just the professor/instructor offering additional time for discussion outside the classroom. The clubs are significant because they offer an experience beyond that classroom that allows you to share information and interact with peers who are in the same pursuit. Through engaging peers beyond the classroom, you can also gauge where you are in your development and find new forms of training or information to close the gap. More exposure outside of the classroom will also generate more opportunities to develop; depending on the situation you could even get job offers. Keep in mind the more immersed you get into this new skillset the better you will become. To truly become good at what you are trying to become, just simply going to class is not good enough. Book knowledge with no application will make you moderate at best. Always remember, you are now spending money (unless you have a scholarship) to learn a skill, it is up to you to learn everything possible and truly get your money's worth. Think of it this way, when investing in anything whether it be a company or a product, you expect a return on investment (a profit); paying to learn a skill is the ultimate investment into yourself (the product); so, ensure that you do what is necessary to get full value of your return on investment.

Now that you are in school, and you are getting immersed with activities that revolve around your desired skill set (major); it is now time to start considering potential companies you want to work for when you graduate. Yes, I know it is early and you just started school; but let's keep in mind the sole reason we are in school is to learn a skill and obtain a job. A lot of people start going to job fairs and applying for jobs in their senior year, some even wait until the last semester of their senior year. At that point, the pressure is on, and you could find yourself just trying to get a job as opposed to the job you want. Some people luck out and still get the job they want. Others, when applying to dream jobs (if your school is not known for that expertise), get passed up because companies have no way to assess your skills coming in. To prevent the last-minute scrambling and to remove some of the pressures associated with balancing school and finding a job thereafter; it would behoove you to pursue internships.

An internship is a temporary assignment at a company. Traditionally they were conducted in the summer between semesters; but now companies offer internships during the semester, there are even internships offered during the winter break. Some companies even go as far as to offer yearly internships. Pursuing and obtaining an internship carries with it many great benefits:

- You will have the opportunity to gain real-time experience performing tasks in your desired skillset, which will allow you to build an effective resume prior to graduation, as well as provide you an edge when entering the work force.

- You will be able to gain a feel for different companies and have an opportunity to determine if you identify with the culture of the company while you still have the luxury of choosing.

- You will be able to determine if this is the skillset that you ultimately want to pursue while you still have time to adjust your plan (you can adjust your plan at any time in life, the goal is to pursue something we are passionate about and want to stick with long term)

- Companies will be able to assess your abilities and potential, as well. Depending on your performance, you can obtain a full-time job that will be waiting for you upon completion of school.

Performing internships throughout your time in school will give you a major edge over your competition upon graduation. By successfully performing internships you already prove that you can perform within the work force environment. Thus, gaining full time experience. With full time experience you now have a story to tell, which can be articulated on a resume. Being able to give real time examples of achievements that you made within that environment will further justify why you deserve an opportunity at the companies you choose to pursue. Businesses expect individuals to be ready to come in and contribute to the overall business and be able to learn the inner workings of the business along the way. Remember, upon graduation you are now competing with people from all walks of life. There is no limit to the competition. Some people have been out of school and working for quite some time; but given your experience you are just as capable of coming in and performing that job than anyone else. Also, depending on how diverse your experience in internships is, it would make you an even more desirable candidate because you have learned multiple ways to obtain the same goals. Therefore, you as a fresh pair of eyes, could contribute to improving daily operations. Ultimately, through internships it gives you experience which makes you competitive amongst experienced workers for a desired job.

When in school pursuing a career, everyone wants to work for the top companies. Everyone dreams of working in the top companies within a specific field or just businesses that everyone is familiar with. It is always an ego boost to say that you work for one of the top companies in the world; but it's another thing to enjoy your job. Some people, not being aware of their options, feel that they are restricted to one company because of how much they are paid. Even though, they do not like the company. Others, who were late in their pursuit of a job, find out that the job they have is not what they thought; therefore, they must look for another job. Depending on their current situation, they may not have the freedom to just walk away from a job. For that reason, they must stay in a place where they are unhappy, until they find another job. Upon accepting an offer to another job, they must begin that evaluation of their environment again. The job they enter may be even worse than the previous. Unfortunately, these are things that may occur in your adult life. I say all that to say, the best way to weigh your options, is through performing in internships. Not only do you gain experience (as mentioned previously), but you also get a feel for the environment. How well do you get along with your peers? How is your relationship with your superiors? How are you treated as a person in your daily interactions? What is the group consensus on feelings toward the company in general? Through an internship you have an opportunity to determine if a company is a good fit for you prior to fully committing to a company. If you perform an internship and you do not like how you feel or how you are treated during that time, it's okay, because you will be going right back to school. Upon your return to school, you can look for another company and perform an internship the next available timeframe. Also, if you do like a company (and the company mutually likes you), you can return to do another internship in a new role. By performing multiple roles in your desired field (major), you now have more solid skills and achievements to list on your resume. Thus, making you more competitive in the job market upon graduation. Just a reminder, the goal is to obtain a position in your field, upon completion of school.

Sometimes, in life we have great dreams and aspirations to do many things. We can study the skills, learn multiple techniques, and practice various simulations. We can even look to famous people as role models, for their ability to perform a skill and all the success that they were able to achieve doing so. But, when we are placed in a position where it is time to apply all the knowledge we have obtained; unfortunately, we realize it is not what we thought. This realization can come, even if you are good at a particular skill. There could be plenty of contributing factors to the understanding that a skill or lifestyle surrounding a job is not for us. It could be the hours associated with a job; the different environments you will have to function in for periods of time; you could even feel that with your skills it can translate over to something more ideal to your needs. There are many reasons to not like a job. The downside to realizing that you do not like a specific career field, is that now you must identify a career you like and begin the process of development again. The upside to realizing that you do not like a specific career field during an internship is you are in a position where changing your pursuits will not have as much of an impact on your life. It is one thing to change your mind while in school, it is another thing to change your mind when you have been working in a career field for years. Especially, when you have bills and a family that depends on you to contribute in order for you all to function efficiently. It is better to change now, while you have less skin in the game. You may or may not delay your graduation, but that is a small price to pay in the pursuit of a career that you will enjoy. What better way to do that than through a temporary assignment? Endure the assignment for the duration of time specified, then move on to start laying the blueprint for your new desired path. Remember the goal at this point is to get the best return on your investment; if you are comfortable and confident that the outcome will improve, investing more time or funds is not a bad thing. Especially, if it will increase your return on investment.

One of the greatest things, in my opinion, that relates to performing internships is the ability to obtain a job with a company you want upon graduation. It is a great feeling to come into a company that you identify with, and you are recognized for your efforts. Not only are you recognized, but they feel that you show so much potential that they can't afford to lose you to any competitors. For that reason, companies will offer interns job positions upon graduation (if certain academic achievements are met). How much of a relief is that? To already know where you are going and what you will be doing when you graduate. Now, the only focus for you is getting grades (which you should already be doing); what a heavy burden lifted off your shoulders. Even better, the company can still utilize internships to continue your development until you arrive on your first official day after graduation.

"The future rewards those who press on. I don't have time to feel sorry for myself. I don't have time to complain. I'm going to press on."

- 44th United States President, Barack Obama

SECOND TIME AROUND

I was in my final semester of college. Looking forward to starting my career because I'm about to finish college with my business degree. Not only was I about to graduate, but I was on track to graduate Summa Cum Laude (grade point average of 3.8 or higher on a 4.0 scale). This is one of the highest awards you can get. For that reason, I knew plenty of companies were going to want to hire me, for sure. Now up to this point, I have just focused solely on sports and grades. I got jobs through temp agencies during the winter and summer breaks; so that I can train for the season and have money when I got back to school. I was confident, because up to that point I was always told "go to school, get a degree and get a job"; I've been sticking to the blueprint, following it to the T. So, of course, it's only right based on the sequence of events that I am about to get a good job. I couldn't have been more wrong.

I didn't realize how difficult finding a job after college was going to be until one random day in school. Something told me to look for some jobs; just to get an idea of all the job options I could actually choose from. My intent was to just simply make a list of jobs so I could research the criteria to apply later. I went online to look for a federal job (everybody always talks about how good federal jobs were). I went on a famous website and started a very general search. I didn't even put in a specific skill set; I just conducted a broad search for jobs in New Jersey (my goal was to go right back home after college). When I entered the search, and I will never forget this, it said "No Jobs Found". I thought, surely this is incorrect, so I tried the search again, same results. What am I going to do?

What are the odds? It just so happened that I decided, with some persuasion from my parents, to get a Business Degree during a time that everyone became motivated to start opening their own businesses. To add to my dismay, I didn't even know what specific roles I was looking for. Clearly, up to this point I had not done my research. I'm stressing at this point; this is not how the blueprint that I was taught was supposed to go. Fortunately, I had a whole semester to figure it out. The pressure was on, and I was up to the challenge.

I applied to numerous jobs, had several interviews and they all ended with variations of the answer no. Despite receiving a no, every company's decision revolved around the same theme; that although I have a great GPA and articulate well, a lot of the entry position personnel entered through internship programs and there was no way to confirm my abilities prior to making a commitment. At the time I was very discouraged, I stopped looking for big time companies and started looking for just any job. Fortunately, by the time I graduated from college, I was able to obtain a job as a guidance counselor at a juvenile detention center. The opposite end of the spectrum from what I just spent my whole college career learning, but I was thankful to have a job. Knowing that was not my end all be all career, a brief 3 months later I found myself doing security work in Washington DC. It wasn't exactly what I wanted to do, but the money was better than I ever had so I felt this is good for the time being. After spending time with all my newfound friends throughout the DMV area and being motivated by their lives at the time; I quickly realized that I am capable of more. But what was more for me?

During my time working as security, I was fortunate enough to work in buildings managed by people who worked in the government. Those people, in my eyes, were extremely successful (especially in comparison to the adults where I grew up). Often at times, I would have brief conversations with them about their background (without being too intrusive); and the one thing the individuals I encountered had in common was prior military service. Then I looked back at men and women in my family that also served in the military, and they were living pretty good, as well. So, in my mind, I felt that the military was a good catalyst to move my career in the right direction. With that being said, I joined the United States Army.

Shortly after joining the Army, I completed a course called the Officer Candidate School and became an Army Officer (a Transportation Officer to be more specific). Not too long after becoming an Officer, I deployed to Afghanistan. This is where I discovered my talent and true passion. During my time in Afghanistan, I oversaw retrograde and redeployment operations. This meant that I managed the logistics that revolved around getting people and equipment from one location to another. During my time in this role, I quickly grasped the concepts and naturally performed the day-to-day operations. I had the luxury of being in a space where I got to interact with subject matter experts (both military and contractors) of all aspects of logistics. I made time to sit with all of them in order to better understand all pieces of the operation to the point where I was able to perform anyone's role if need be. Not only did I have a desire to do a good job while in Afghanistan, I developed a passion for logistics; I was good at it and wanted to learn more procedures and techniques that revolved around the skill set (discovering your passion more sooner than later). After some discussions with a good friend back home, I understood that graduate school was the best way to acquire the additional knowledge that I was seeking.

I started researching schools that focused on logistics and supply chain. This was somewhat a difficult task because I was still in Afghanistan, so I did not have the ability to verify the information with campus visits; I had to find statistics and sources to confirm the statistics. After narrowing it down to 3 schools and working through a rigorous application process (because all my references were in another country at the time); I secured a full-academic scholarship to attend North Carolina Agricultural and Technical State University and started graduate school less than 2 months after returning from Afghanistan.

Before I even arrived at the school, I already had a goal in mind; I am going to school to learn about logistics and I'm going to get a job in that field. I had a different level of focus; I was in clubs, I was talking to teachers, and I had a graduate assistant role in order to do additional research outside of my schoolwork. Everything I did from the moment I stepped foot on campus revolved around logistics. Not only did I learn logistics, but graduate school showed me that logistics was merely one piece of the puzzle. From there I was introduced to supply chain and learned how to look at an operation in its entirety. Also, from my experience in undergrad, I knew that all these things I'm learning were good; but it means nothing if nobody knows I possess it. I must put myself in a space where I can apply it. What better way to do that than to apply for an internship? Yes, I was older and had experience now, but sometimes in life you must take a step back to reposition yourself to move forward. Before the end of my first school year, I acquired an internship with one of the largest oil companies in the world. I did such a good job in my internship, that I was offered a full-time position that was scheduled to start upon my completion of graduate school.

What a relief to know that all that effort I was putting in was not in vain. My thoughts and actions were oriented towards one thing, I refused to be distracted. Now all I had to do was continue learning and prepare for my transition. I graduated with honors. Mission Accomplished!

"It is up to you to bring yourself to the attention of powerful people around you. They're not going to find you on their own."

- Richard Parsons

Building A Network

We have transitioned from college and found a job that aligns with our skill sets and possesses an environment that we can be comfortable in. Great, your foot is in the door. Some may think this is the most important part; however, it is what you do once you are brought into a company that will dictate your future with that company. A lot of people come in with a full head of steam and give the job 110%. They are so concerned with making a good impression that they go above and beyond to make sure that they do everything perfectly. That is a good mentality to have; but everyone knows nothing is perfect. What you don't want to do is come in performing at a level that you cannot sustain. By doing that, you set a level of expectations that management will have for you. Once you burn yourself out and begin to throttle back; in their eyes, you can appear to be underperforming. So, the first thing you want to focus on is generating a level of understanding with your manager on what their expectations are for an individual in that role. By having this discussion with your manager in the beginning, you now know your left and right limits, as well as what level of effort is needed to deliver what is required of you. This initial conversation that you have with your manager is crucial to having success early on in your position. To reiterate what was stated previously, through this conversation you are gaining a clear understanding of your role and what your manager's expectations of you are. Through gaining an understanding of your role, you now have a better picture of how you contribute to the business and what areas of development you should focus on. Furthermore, by understanding what areas you need to focus on, in relation to your skills acquired during school and your internships, you can now start to get an idea of how much effort you will need to put into being successful at your job. During your assessment it is cool to identify what tasks will be easy versus what tasks may pose a bit of difficulty. By finding these areas of difficulty early on, you can start to look for resources to improve yourself in those areas; whether it be material or subject matter experts within the company who are willing to walk you through the steps in those identified areas. You want to be as proactive as possible. Also, by reaching out and communicating to people within the company, you start to build relationships within the workplace. You also create a name for yourself because people that observe you execute what has been taught, as well as how you carry yourself; will be more comfortable working with you. Being pleasant to work with is a good trait to have associated with your name, especially when just starting out within a company. And understand, EVERYONE, is observing you.

Another piece of vital information that is obtained from your initial conversation with your manager is who you work with and who you must provide products/ data to within the company. It is important to get an understanding of what and who your role impacts in the business. By obtaining an understanding of that, it opens the door for more conversations with other individuals within the company. Especially, people who you will have to interact with in your everyday operations. By generating those initial conversations, you create an open line of communication that will prove to be very helpful; especially, in the beginning stages for you at the company.

During the conversations with these individuals, there are several pieces of information that you want to gain from those conversations. The things you want to obtain from the conversation are:

- **What is it that they do.**

- **What information do they utilize from you in order to do their job.**

- **Who do they provide their portion of the work to.**

Learning what the individuals you will be interacting with during daily operations is important to your development in your role, as well as career projection within the company. Learning what the others do around you gives you a better picture of the overall structure of the company. Knowledge of the overall structure will assist you in your day-to-day operations because it will tell you who requires what information. Knowing who does what can also enable you to plan for future positions after you have successfully completed your initial role within the company. Once you have a grasp on your role and the work required of you; understanding the work output and criteria for other jobs within the company, allows you to research where your gaps are in order to prepare for career progression in the company. Understanding what people do is also important when navigating the company; because you do not want to position yourself for a role that will not be ideal for you, as well. This can also improve future conversations with your manager; because eventually they will ask you what kind of roles you are looking to enter next if the opportunity presented itself. From your prior knowledge and interactions, you can give them an idea; this will show that you are committed to the company and that you are considering them long term.

Understanding what information is utilized from the work you provide is crucial to your overall performance. By knowing what information is required from you, this allows you to shape your day and gives you an idea of what will require more of your energy and time. Some work that you create might also call for frequent collaboration, as well. Depending on who you must work with to complete objectives, may require more time than others. You want to be mindful of this because you don't want to consume so much of your time working with certain individuals, that you miss deadlines for other work that would be easy to accomplish. Time management is a major skill that managers look at while you are performing within a role. Another important factor that you learn through those conversations are if work that was done in the past is no longer utilized, that is still being performed. These discoveries can generate additional dialogue with your manager. Your manager can be extremely busy and may not be aware of every aspect of what you do; that is your job. When you come across information of that nature, you want to bring it to the attention of your manager before adjusting your workload. They may be fully aware that information is not utilized by the individuals you work with, but it may be utilized in other ways that you are not aware of. If they weren't aware, you just took one thing off your plate and gained more time to utilize for other tasks. These conversations will ultimately improve you and your manager's relationship, because you show your manager that you will keep them in the loop with things that pertain to their scope of the business. They are more willing to work with you if they can trust you.

Knowing who the people you collaborate with, submit their work/ report to, is essential in developing a better understanding of the business in its entirety. In addition to understanding, it gives you the opportunity to do two things; **1.** Identify more people that you should generate relationships with within the business; **2.** Allows you to amend your career track. These two things will allow you to fine tune your strategy in your day-to-day operations; as well as ensure you are more intentional about your interactions within the company.

Initiating and building business relationships with individuals higher in rank within a company is pertinent to your advancement within a company. As you generate these relationships, ensure you keep them professional, and you are communicating your goals and intentions during those conversations. This is not to necessarily be their buddy; because they are of higher rank than you; but more so to become relevant within the company. Of course, your work will speak for itself; but it speaks volumes when others mention you in conversations that you are not privy to. Managers and supervisors engage in talent meetings at all levels, and they are constantly strategizing on ways to improve the overall performance of the business. When opportunities arise, and your name is mentioned, the more people who are familiar with you and your performance, the less advocating that needs to be made for a collective decision to be made. Also, by forming relationships with individuals who have been in a company for a long time, it gives the opportunity for mentoring. Keep in mind, we have entered an environment that is extremely different than that of where we were growing up. Some of the actions and decisions that were influenced by our elders growing up may not be suitable or have a positive outcome in this new environment. Also, we have surpassed the people guiding us in our youth; it will call for a new mindset and new guidance. When entering a new territory, it would behoove you to establish a relationship with a person who is knowledgeable of the land. Who better to do that, than managers and supervisors who have already established tenure within a company? Establishing relationships with people in higher positions within a company who have an interest in your success within the company is the ultimate key to building a network within a company.

When entering a company your manager has the expectations that you will have a 5-year plan for goals and aspirations within the company. Along with achievements you should also have an idea of what positions you would like to pursue (they should build off your previous position). This is also why it is important to know who the individuals you collaborate with report to and what their roles are within the company. By doing this you can then start to develop a career/action plan which ultimately enables you to stay on track as you progress through the ranks of a company. Knowing multiple roles and the roles that would follow allows you to lay out what additional training/ knowledge you need to obtain in order to qualify for the next role. You want to ensure that the additional training you are seeking ties into what you are trying to do next. You want to avoid putting effort into training that's not beneficial and overlooking training that is necessary for qualifying for the next targeted position. Although, to succeed in life you must be a lifelong learner; you want to make sure that your efforts are in alignment with the phases of your plan. Ensure that your additional training is building upon the experience you have currently have. Work smarter not harder.

"Hold on to your dreams of a better life and stay committed to striving to realize it."

- Earl G Graves, Sr.

Civilian VS. Military Transition

From having the opportunity to have worked in the largest oil company in the world, as well as work in the Army; I can tell you that career progression is quite different. In the military, you are given a job that falls in line with your job skill and rank. Once, you are given your assignment; you go to the location and perform your job until you are contacted by the career officer and provided with a new assignment. While in a position, there is no one else at your place of work that performs your job, so the stress of competing for a role is not present. You simply report to your new location and perform that role. You don't have much say over where your next role is; it is up to your career officer to align you with your next role and ensure that your work experience is progressing. The career counselor must also ensure that as you progress, you work within your skillsets for that intended rank. What actually dictates the speed of your career progression is your ability to meet the standards dictated by the military to qualify for the next rank. These standards come in the form of successfully performing key roles for a specified amount of time, in addition to completing specific military courses that are outlined by your rank and skillset. Seems fair enough; however, everything in the military is team based. Therefore, your ability to perform your daily tasks are based on your relationships with other personnel. There are not too many tasks that you can complete by yourself. Often at times you will be interacting with personnel that are at a higher rank than you, as well as individuals at a lower rank. So, your ability to communicate effectively is also crucial to your success; and how you treat the people you interact with. People are more willing to help if you come with respect, in a timely manner. Being friendly and successfully accomplishing your daily tasks are keys to being successful at your job; but always be mindful that in order to be promoted within the military you must complete the mandatory schools. You can be great at your job, and everyone can like you, but if you don't qualify (meet the army standards) for your next role, you will not progress. In the military, lack of progression overtime is just as bad as not being able to perform a job.

In the civilian world career progression is dramatically different. When working in a company, they are hiring you for a very specific role. They don't necessarily plan your career progression or even have intentions for you to move up within the company. After proving you can perform your role, they intended on you to have; the speed in which progress after that is solely up to you. After building a relationship with your supervisor and having the discussion of your career goals within the company, your supervisor should direct you to other individuals to have conversations and form relationships with. If not your supervisor, then an individual who has agreed to be your mentor. As you begin to form relationships with other individuals within the company, you will discuss your achievements in your current role, as well as things you are doing outside of your role to develop. With those things in mind, as opportunities for new roles present themselves within a company, your supervisor and or those key individuals you have formed relationships with will tell you about them and recommend you apply for those roles. Normally, the supervisor for the new role will be an individual you have formed a relationship with. They have monitored your performance for some time and verified your success through discussions with your supervisor, who most likely is their peer or subordinate. In lieu of those relationships, they won't really recommend opportunities to you if they don't feel they align with your skillsets or your goals that you have mentioned in your conversations with them. Something to keep in mind in career progression in the civilian world, 9 times out of 10 the roles within the company aren't posted until they already have someone in mind for the role. For this reason, it is important to understand what you want to do and build relationships with people who are within that space. It is not impossible, but it could be difficult to obtain a new role within a company if nobody in that department is familiar with you.

One thing that is dramatically different with the military vs. civilian world is the control your supervisor has over your career. As stated earlier, in the military a career counselor manages your career; in the civilian world, your supervisor manages your career. What I mean by this is, in the military your supervisor evaluates how you perform in your current role, and you supervisor's manager evaluates your potential based on how well you performed your role; but they do not determine where you go or what you do next. In the military you are given a role with a predetermined amount of time that you will perform that role; and based off your performance in that role, the career counselor will determine what and where your next role will be. You are allowed to make a wish list, in terms of where you would like to work, but ultimately it is up to the needs of the military. Now on the flipside, in the civilian world, your supervisor may have a say in how long you stay in a role; but typically, there are no timelines for individuals within a given role at a company. You can work in a position for as long as your company wants to have you. With you in a position successfully performing, that is one less position they have to worry about filling. Also, if you are performing well in a role, a supervisor might not be willing to part ways with you to allow you to progress within a company. Yes, this does happen at times, especially when you are young and just entering the workforce. You don't want to mentally get into a place where you feel stuck or trapped; that feeling can carry over into your performance and decrease your output overtime. Also, you don't want to get too affixed on the money as a reason to stay, because your job is not guaranteed (companies downsize and reorganize all the time). With this in mind, if career progression is something you desire, and your work relationships are not creating opportunities for you; it may call for you to apply for roles outside of your company. But I will discuss this later in the book.

"Show me a successful individual and I'll show you someone who had real positive influences in his or her life. I don't care what you do for a living – if you do it well I'm sure there was someone cheering you on or showing the way. A mentor."

- Denzel Washington

Mentors vs. Role Models

Our society today really does a good job of highlighting successful people. Every time you turn around, the media is broadcasting a new achievement that an individual has accomplished. During these times when these successful people's accomplishments are highlighted, you will often see multiple interviews being held relating to their newfound achievement. And during these interviews, these people are asked different things relating to their thought process during the time that they were accomplishing this goal. Did you notice, at some point in the interview, the successful person will always give some words of encouragement to people so that they can be motivated to achieve the same things. And those words always revolve around the theme of following your dreams. Which is a great driver, and a reminder that anything can be achieved through hard work and seizing the right opportunities. I, for one, am thankful for those uplifting words and them being living examples; but motivation is a small fraction of what is needed to develop a blueprint. It's rare to find these successful people get into the specifics, share specific exercises they do, or strategies utilized to improve their performance. Then again, that is how they maintain success in their industry/ career.

How about we touch closer to home. Remember those older people in your neighborhood, that in comparison to everyone else, they just appeared to be more successful than everybody around them. We are all in the same environment and have access to the same resources, but it appears that they have some sort of edge over everyone else. Some of the individuals' choices of employment were not positive, but I am referring to the individuals with good legal careers. Everyone knows those families; the ones that get invites to come to talk schools and after school programs, those type of individuals. I was always curious how or what these individuals, who lived in the same environment as me, did to make themselves so much further ahead or successful. Like, is there something here that I don't know about? Am I missing something, what am I not doing that they are doing? And as children, teenagers, we use to go up to them or in the programs (because there is always a Q & A session) and ask them what they did to reach that type of status or level in this area. Then often more than not, the individuals give the same statement or something close to "if you work really hard and stay focused you can achieve this too". I understand that, and I thought at the time (in my youth) that the work I was doing was hard, at least to me. So, I felt that maybe I needed to work harder at what I was doing. They never get into the actual process that led up to where they are now. They may touch on some experiences, but never what they did and why. Besides Q & A sessions are not the space for them to get in depth anyway.

Or I'll give one more example, when you do find what you feel is your first career job. You network and find a manager that performs within your field. You spend time getting to know this manager and expressing your goals. This manager even takes the time to show you the things they have acquired through their success with the company. The office, the car, other random materialistic things. They always tell you "if you work really hard, you can achieve this too". For some, just the thought of having the ability to acquire those things is enough motivation for them. The idea that one day they too can have those very things and motivate young impressionable minds with the thought of also acquiring those things. However, when opportunities arise, the manager never speaks up on your behalf. They never lay out milestones for you, additional training you should seek to improve your overall performance. These individuals are spending time with you, but never facilitate an opportunity for you to advance within the company. These types of individuals are what you would call role models.

When dealing with a role model the majority of scenarios have a common theme, and that is motivation. We see the fruits of their labor and believe we can achieve these things too. How often do younger people set a goal because they are inspired by a successful person they observed. The relation to that person manifests a dream and because you are viewing it in present day, you know it can be done. Yes, you very well could be the next success story; but how often do we see talented people in unfortunate situations. How many times have you heard, "if I just got that opportunity". How many times have we seen those individuals that have so much motivation, enthusiasm, tenacity, but no guidance. All of that potential bottled up or being utilized to benefit everyone but themselves, leaving an individual stagnant. When they reach out to people who act like they have their genuine interest in mind, but in reality, they are being led further away from their goals than when they started. Even worse, they delay that individuals progress because they have them doing things that have nothing to do with their growth in that desired skillset. Then to add insult to injury don't even inform them of opportunities that they are fully aware of. These individuals will spend time with you, have fun with you, but never provide the guidance you need. Despite these possibilities, the fact remains, you need people to progress in life. The difficult part is understanding who is truly in your corner and who is stringing you along. What you don't want to have happen is that you put your faith in someone or a group with the hopes that they will eventually assist in your growth; then after a period of time you realize you are still in the same spot. When you interact with or observe individuals in a position in life that you are working to obtain and they never provide you guidance or an idea of things you should be striving towards, these are role models.

Role models are exactly what their name entails. A model, they reflect an image that people want to obtain. They may live a lifestyle or possess materialistic things that appeal to you. Others, have positions or titles that people are striving to achieve. Role models are just as important to your network as actual mentors. With knowing certain people, it now exposes you to things that others are not privy to. It might be things that exist that you aren't even aware of until you meet this person; so, having a relationship with a role model is not a waste. However, you must be realistic about what type of impact these individuals are having in your life and how much time you are investing in those relationships. To determine if you are dealing with someone who can be considered a role model, you must be mindful of what results from your interactions with this person. If this individual is simply showing you things, but not taking the time to explain to you how this was obtained or created (especially if you ask); this individual could be considered a role model. Another thing to be mindful of is discussing events whether they be past, present or future; pay attention to how many of those activities relate to what you have communicated to them you are trying to do and how many of them you were informed of. If the event was open to anyone and it took place during the time that you knew the individual, you should begin limiting your time with this individual or placing them in another category of associates. You have to limit your time because they are not as interested in your growth as you assume them to be. It takes little to no effort to inform someone of something taking place, especially if you know it relates to their ambitions. I don't want to go as far as to say they have evil intentions for you, but they may simply just be more concerned with their own growth, rightfully so. There is nothing wrong with that. Just be mindful that when you are setting time for personal growth, that is not the individual that should be considered in that time.

We often get role models confused for mentors and we can find ourselves wasting a lot of valuable time. Mentors are like role models; but the key difference is, they are taking an active role in your growth, in your career and as a person. Once you express interest or seek guidance from an individual that is further along in their career, and you hope to obtain that level of success one day, you must ensure they agree to the request; and that they are actively participating. Actively participating means scheduling time with you to discuss goals and ways to achieve those goals. They should then follow up with you and check on your progress achieving these goals. Another thing a mentor should be doing is introducing or recommending you reach out to other individuals. By doing this they understand the direction you are trying to go and is assisting you in building a network that revolves around your goals. Having more than one mentor is a good thing and can only result in making you a more well-rounded candidate for opportunities within your company or career field.

When dealing with an actual mentor, you will discover there are two types of mentors. There is one that tells you what to do, and one that steers your choices based off their knowledge and experience and perspective of your performance throughout the relationship. Both types of mentorships are beneficial to your growth but based on the tactics one chooses to utilize it can move your career in different ways. Both methods will allow you to progress; however, one style you are following in an individual's footsteps and the other is allowing you to develop yourself and expand your options. I like to call these two types of mentor styles; I can get you here; and let's see where the road takes you. Again, you can't go wrong with either method; however, you must understand yourself and what is beneficial to you.

The "I can get you here" mentorship style is a beneficial and straight forward style that has good pros and cons. Some of those factors to keep in mind in relation to this method is:

- This individual is coaching you to get to where they currently are
- You will be given the blueprint according to what worked for them
- There is not much room for flexibility in relation to the plan

- If you determine you have a new end goal, their guidance may no longer be beneficial

The "I can get you here" mentor is a great mentor to have. They are not concerned or intimidated by your progression. By not seeing you as potential competition, they are more inclined to help you grow within a company. Businesses that are ideal for this type of mentorship usually reflect a somewhat bureaucratic work structure. In better terms, a company where your promotion is not only determined by your level of success, but time within a specific position. You cannot move up within this structure until you have worked in a position for a specified amount of time. This type of structure reflects that of the military or government entities. Since they don't have to be concerned with you potentially being their competition, the more senior individuals are more inclined to assist with your career progression. With this style of mentorship, they have determined through your interaction that you do have potential and they want you to follow in their footsteps.

This form of mentorship is essential because their guidance to you is based off what has already worked for them. They have already gone through the aches and pains of the journey and know what needs to be done. They also, through trial and error, know what needs to be avoided. By following their guidance/instructions; it makes the path for you more efficient. Keep in mind, efficient does not mean easy. You will still have to meet and exceed the standard with every task given. Efficient, as it relates to this situation, means that every action you take is more effective because it will directly impact your goal; and you avoid wasting time on things that you thought were helping but really weren't. Success is the result of traveling the road less traveled; so, if a person who has already traveled that road is genuinely willing to guide you, **LISTEN**.

The downside to this style of mentorship is that there is not much flexibility in the plan. The individual who is guiding you only knows what worked for them. In some unfortunate circumstances, a situation that should have worked out for them, didn't. Instead of accepting defeat, they had to adjust and commit to another way to achieve their goals. As a result, they may see a method or course of action as one that should be avoided. As they guide you, they are more so giving you instructions. If you choose to not follow their instructions or want to try other things, their mentorship is less effective. In this style of mentorship, you must understand your left and right limits are based off the experiences your mentor encountered along their journey. As you already know, not everyone in life starts in the same place; and everyone doesn't have the same motivation or determination. For this reason, you must decide within yourself if you are up for the challenges/tasks presented to you by your mentor and if so, commit to the plan.

As stated previously, if you choose to not follow their instructions, their mentorship is less effective. In the "I can get you there" style of mentorship, it's hard to help an individual if they choose not to follow the instructions/guidance given. The more an individual deviates from what they are told, the less influence the mentor has over your success. Another thing that may come from that situation is, if you deviate from your mentor's instructions, your course of action may have a less than ideal outcome. As your results become less ideal, you are still coming to your mentor for guidance. This makes things difficult for your mentor as well because you have asked them to be committed to your success. If you get into a season in your career, where you are receiving instructions from your mentor and you are actively deciding that you are going to do something else; then they are no longer mentoring you, but merely making recommendations. At the end of the day, you are responsible for your own future and following another individual's guidance is a choice; but if you decide that you want to move in another direction, don't consume your mentor's time. Also, let them know what your new plan is, to avoid unnecessary frustration.

The "Let's see where the road takes you" is another style of mentorship that is a little more vague, but still beneficial when utilized properly. Some of the factors to keep in mind with this style of mentorship is:

- For Individuals who seek progression, but not sure what they ultimately want to do

- Intended for individuals who are more flexible and open to change

- Depending on the outcome of each phase may result in frequent changing of mentors

The "Let's see where the road takes you" is a great style of mentorship to utilize when just entering the workforce. Especially, if you are in some sort of development program that focuses on you experiencing different aspects of a business prior to sending you down a specific career path. Individuals who agree to mentor an individual under these conditions are focused on getting the best output from an individual in their current state. This mentor is typically your direct supervisor who can confirm that you are meeting or exceeding the standard. They are able to do this because they are interacting and observing you more frequently than others. Also, your performance directly impacts theirs. By displaying your ability to meet or exceed the standard this will show that you can take on more responsibility; as well as allow the mentor to show their ability to develop others. Mentoring you is mutually beneficial for both parties. The way this individual mentors you is by communicating what they would like to actively see you doing in order to achieve the standard. If you are already achieving the standard, they look to find ways that you can build on the skills that you are already displaying, or things you can do in addition to add to your set of skills. The most important thing to keep in mind when dealing with this type of mentorship is to understand that the end goal is not predetermined in this relationship. The goal in this type of mentorship is to ensure you as the mentee are advancing within the company and not staying stagnant.

"Let's see where the road takes you" mentorship is better oriented towards individuals who are flexible and open to change. An individual who is talented and shows a lot of potential, but not yet firm on their end goal would benefit more from this style of mentorship. As your mentor interacts with you and further assesses your performance and potential based on your response to feedback; your mentor may be able to make recommendations on what avenues to pursue next in your transition. If they are knowledgeable of the company and can relate your personality and performance with the managers in other departments their recommendation may be the best option for your development in the company. Their assessment of you may be able to open your mind to possibilities that you may have never considered. Also, the feedback that you are receiving from them may require you to change your course of action and focus your energy on other aspects of the job. You may feel you are strong in area, but through mentorship you may find out you could be better. Another example is you may focus too heavily in one area but are not developing as much in others. Based off mentorship you discover that you have to redistribute your energy in a more balanced manner. Your ability to take feedback (criticism), make the adjustments and improve your performance will take you far. Now through mentorship you have demonstrated that you are coachable as well. Demonstrating the ability to be coached in this style of mentorship is a tremendous strength that will benefit you throughout your career, wherever you decide to be. Through their mentorship they will develop you into a more well-rounded performer, thus making you prepared for whatever avenue you choose to go next.

With the fast results that stem from the "Let's see where the road takes you" mentorship; there is a downside to it as well. With this style of mentorship, it is only for specific periods and or phases of your career. As a result, the "Let's see where the road takes you" mentorship will cause you to have to change mentors frequently. The multiple changing of mentors forces you to have to adjust to multiple personalities. That initial analysis of your mentor as well as them analyzing you must take place before you can make any guided progress in your development. Flexibility and the ability to adapt is crucial and depending on where your talents take you may call for you to change more frequently than you may desire. Progression isn't easy, but you must do what needs to be done and be genuine about it.

Another downside to the "Let's see where the road takes you" mentorship style, is that you may not like where the road takes you. At times you will feel that you are heading in a certain direction; but it does not always work out that way. Yes, you will continue to develop, and you will progress; however, you must work for a span of time in a position that may not be desired. When you are in a position that is not necessarily ideal; or you feel that the position is not conducive to your progress, that is the best position for you. We call these types of positions broadening assignments. You may not understand how or why your mentor recommended you to a position such as that; but it is for growth. In the long run you will be thankful because it made you a more rounded candidate for future roles within your company or career.

With both types of mentorship styles, keep in mind the individual you are interacting with is here to help you grow; but it is not beneficial if you do not receive their message and intent positively. Always keep in mind regardless of where your relationship takes you; this individual is trying to help you develop. The last thing you want to do with an individual who is genuinely trying to help you, is to damage that relationship.

"There is no such thing as failure. Failure is just life trying to move us in another direction."

- Oprah Winfrey

NEVER GET TIME BACK

When I was on the brink of graduating from undergrad, I was in hot pursuit of job. Preferably a job that could lead to a career. I was reaching out to more established individuals who I interacted with frequently. There was one guy, who was referred to me from a family member. I reached out and informed the gentlemen that I was interested in working in the establishment that he was in. After speaking with him multiple times over the span of a month, he set up a time for me to meet him. We met multiple times and I even participated in several non-profit events that he held through his organization. He finally agreed to give me an interview. I took a 3-hour drive and stayed at a relative's house the night prior to prepare for my interview. When I arrived and provided my resume, we began the interview. The interview lasted almost an hour and I felt confident because I had no issues with my answers, and I was familiar with the company (did my research). To my dismay, after the interview he provided me with some feedback; that's when he informed me that my resume was good, but he wasn't too familiar with the college I went to. He further went on to say, had I done an internship with the company then they [he] would have been able to confirm my abilities matched my GPA (3.82).

I was devastated. The first real interview I ever had, and I was denied. The justification was what really hurt. I didn't have the luxury of going to a big-time school, but the education that was provided to me at my institution was very solid. At the time my initial feeling was discouragement. I didn't want to continue to overextend myself and utilize my time to benefit others, just to get burned on the back end. During that time, with the young mind frame I possessed; I felt like I was used and strung along. Then the individual justified not giving me an opportunity based on not having familiarity with my school. At that time, I felt that all the well-known companies were going to feel the same way regarding the university I went to. The harder part about the situation was that I focused so much on forming a relationship with that individual, that I did not effectively network. That experience discouraged me from wanting to apply to other competitive companies at that time. I convinced myself, prematurely, that I was wasting time trying to shoot for big time companies because everyone in the field that I was pursuing would not be tracking my school. Not knowing in my youth, that you will have to apply to a lot of jobs and cannot be discouraged. You are going to get a lot of "Nos" in your time; but it only takes that one "Yes". Someone who sees you will recognize your talent and want you as part of their company.

A few years later I decided to enlist in the Army; I crossed paths with an uncle of mine who was significantly high in rank within the Army. Upon his discovery of my interest in the Army; he quickly began to motivate and guide my chosen career path. We spoke almost daily and of course with him being family, I visited him multiple times. My uncle then informed me, based on our interaction and my background (degree, college athlete, and positive personality) he recommended that if I were to join the Army that I pursue the route of a commissioned officer. Without any prior knowledge of that path, he began to inform me of the different career paths within the Army. He then began to instruct me on what criteria I needed to meet, as well as the requirements I needed to obtain prior to applying for such a career path. Once I obtained all the requirements and provided them to the recruiters I was later selected to go to a very selective prestigious training (Officer Candidate School) shortly after completing basic training. My uncle then told me "If you complete the training, let me know". A tad thrown back by the "if", but I was in too deep at this point. Several months later I completed the school. I let my uncle know right away. He allowed me about a good fifteen minutes of celebration and then he said "OK, now it's time to go to work, if you follow my directions, I can get you to where I'm at; but if you want to do your own thing, I can't help you". Again, me being in too deep, I followed his guidance. He walked me through every step, what job skill to choose (based on my background); what schools to enroll in (military has training beyond basic); even instructed me to volunteer for a deployment (which I also did). From there I became more marketable than I could ever imagine. I returned from Afghanistan with a full academic scholarship to graduate school (based on my GPA from my previous school). While in grad school I stayed in the Army and continued working while in graduate school. Companies were finding me and contacting me asking if I was interested in working for them and I hadn't even finished school yet. While in school my uncle still guided me on what additional schools I needed to enroll in; as well as what positions I needed to obtain while in the military to make myself competitive against my peers. He guided my path every step of the way and the amount of progression that I made in life in such a small-time frame blew my mind. It took several years, but in the big scheme of life 3-5 years can literally set you up for a lifetime. It just took the right person to take interest in me and me to be willing to have faith in their guidance.

"Never be limited by other people's limited imaginations."

- Dr. Mae Jemison

TIME TO MAKE MOVES

Have you been in a job where you have been giving it your all; but you just feel that you are not progressing? Are you the individual that everyone comes to for assistance and you contribute to the overall success of your section/department; but when roles of greater responsibility are presented, you are never considered? You have been working in a position for a significant amount of time and desire more pay, but a raise is not considered for the current position you are in. It may appear that you have reached your ceiling; by ceiling I mean, this is as far as you are able to progress within a company. If you are an individual who desires to continue to progress in your career and you are not comfortable where you are in life. In these types of situations where you feel you are starting to become stagnant; it is time for you to start exploring your options.

In life you are going to have to accept 2 things, especially when pursuing a career. The first thing is that life is not fair; and the second thing is your progression in a company is based off the benefits you provide others, not yourself. While in a job, there will be many cases where you are going to get the short end of the stick. There may be a position that you want, you may even compete for the position, but someone else is going to get that position. In some cases, it is who you know, or the perspective of what leaders look for within a company, which will impact the outcome of a lot of decisions. However, in some cases, you get passed over for positions because you are the best at what you do. There is no one within the team that performs that role at the same level as you. When this is the case, you never have to worry about losing your job, because you are too much of an asset; however, they can't afford to move you because they will lose that experience and output. Depending on the type of job you have, when they hire you, the only consideration they have is for the specific role you are selected for. They have no intentions on moving you elsewhere. They are selecting you because their goal is to create a team with the ability to achieve certain goals. This happens often at start-ups and when companies create a new task force/department. The company is looking to create a foundation and unfortunately, you have found yourself there ... the bottom for which the company will utilize to build upon. In these cases, you will find that the best course of action if you are unable to obtain the promotion you are looking for, it is time to apply for roles of higher responsibility outside the company.

If you find yourself in a position like mentioned above, where they have an ideal spot for you and never envisioned moving you elsewhere; you must be mindful of how you move in this potential transition period. I would say ultimately, after being passed over for two roles or an opportunity where you are clearly outperforming the other candidates within that space; it is now time to start looking for other roles outside the company. What you don't want to do during that time is become combative (because of disappointment) or more aggressive in obtaining positions and advocating for roles within the company. Those approaches can ruffle a lot of feathers and now bring unwanted attention to yourself. When you bring unwanted attention to yourself, you make it known that you are no longer happy in the position that you are in. When they see you are no longer happy in your position, but like we said earlier, in their mind they have a predetermined position for you; this company is now most likely going to start to look to replace you (unless your knowledge and performance is just that much more superior). When leaving a company, you always want to leave on your own terms and never before you are ready. So, what you must do during these times is lock into work, but in your off time begin researching other jobs. You still want to perform to your level of expertise, because if you start to pullback this will also bring you on the radar and they will start to become concerned with your lack of performance, as well. The key focus during this time is maintaining a source of income until you find a company to transition to. The worst thing you can do is get terminated from lack of performance before you find another job. Especially, when you are currently within a company where you are seen as an asset in the role you currently are in. I know it can get discouraging knowing that a company is not willing to allow you to surpass your current level; but you still have responsibilities outside of work; and your growth does not stop because of someone else's decisions. Keep your head down, keep showing up, and just prepare yourself so that you can be ready to receive your next opportunity.

Another big thing to be focused on is when you see a shift in energy towards you at work. These shifts can be anything from the amount of work you are receiving, to interaction with coworkers, to interactions with your boss. If you sense people who you had pleasant interactions with in the past now have a lot of tension or friction with you when you engage them. Or possibly you find yourself constantly repeating yourself on the simplest tasks; even worse, your work is misplaced/misinterpreted by members of your team. Attempt to rectify matters with the individual directly. If you are unable to find a solution amongst each other, get your manager involved and observe the type of support you receive from your manager. If it appears that you are not being heard, they attempt to downplay the situation, or they collectively determine that you are the root cause of the issues; it may be time to start looking for new employment elsewhere. You want to be in a space where you are accepted and respected. If you find yourself fighting to convince people to accept/approve of you and your performance, that is nowhere for you to be. Fighting to stay in an establishment such as that can negatively impact your career; rather it be lack of progress, false or downplayed performance evaluations or even worse unjustifiable termination. At times while you find yourself trying to convince people that your intentions are pure, they may already have their mind made up about you. Unfortunately, not all leaders/ managers are good. Not every manager possesses the qualities of a good manager, and some people carry pre-conditioned bias that are just based off their upbringing and there is nothing you can do to change their perspective. If you find yourself in a that predicament where you are working harder at convincing people to like you or accept you than the work, you were hired for; it may be time to consider looking for new employment.

One of the dark sides of dealing with adversity in the workplace is discrimination. Sad to say, some people can just not like you on the strength of you simply being you. Sometimes it has nothing to do with you, but the upbringing of certain individuals has conditioned them to not be fond of certain types of people. In some unfortunate circumstances, certain individuals, especially ones that are in a position of influence, act on those beliefs in a way that is detrimental to the individual or group they target. A lot of people always resort to race, which is a very prevalent thing in today's world; however, an individual can be discriminated against as a result of not only race, but sex, age, sexual preference, religion and even for serving in the military. There are plenty of other categories, but these are the ones that come up often. If you ever find yourself in any of these unfortunate situations, you want to ensure that you are documenting those events. If you have proof through email or written communication between you in the individuals involved, save them. If you and multiple people experience an event together, talk with the individuals and see if they are willing to write statements reflecting the events that occur (rare, but worth a try). Also, if you notice you are constantly being painted in a negative light, in spite of good performance; ensure that you have proof of your performance and document the behavior of the individual treating you less than. When you gather this information, it may seem extreme, but you may want to seek legal advice prior to reporting it to the human resources department within your company. A lot of people have the misconception that human resources work on behalf of the employees; however, human resources work for the betterment and protection of the company. What this means is, even if an event occurs and the individual is completely in the wrong; the human resources job is to resolve the matter in the most efficient and effective way possible. This means what course of action can be taken that won't bring attention to the company or cost them money. For these reasons, you want to seek legal advice and have representation when you approach human resources about the situation. Especially, when you see that the situation cannot be resolved with a simple conversation. Also, seeking legal advice before you approach the situation within the company keeps the focus off you. Sometimes bad people just want to make you miserable when you share an environment; but you can endure (if you have the resiliency to do so) a situation until you transition somewhere else. Also, the legal counsel you seek may inform you that despite the unfortunate circumstances, the matter is not significant enough to escalate. This will also help you avoid unwanted attention. Unfortunately, it may be a matter that must be endured for a period of time until you transition to a new role or company. What you don't want to happen is you escalate the matter, and you don't have enough evidence or human resources determines the best course of action would be to terminate you. While you are collecting evidence to justify your claim, they are coaching the individual you are dealing with to build a case against you. This is the sad downside of business; but you must be aware. I hope that you never find yourself in that predicament; however, you must know how to act if the event ever occurs. So again, I reiterate, seek legal advice before you approach the human resources department within your company.

At any point in life, you must understand that jobs come and go. Also, not every company is for you. Keep in mind just because something is not working or didn't work in one company does not mean you were not meant to work in that field. It does not mean that you are not meant for that craft. What it means is that the individuals there did not value your efforts or you as an individual. At times your determination and progress can be intimidating to those that are around you.

You want to be able to recognize when you are seen as a threat as opposed to an asset. Understand, this is no fault of your own. Not every company or environment is conducive to your growth. It is more beneficial for you to discover this early in your career where transitions won't impact you as much; in comparison to later in your career when you are more invested in your situation. At all times ensure that you are investing and saving while in a company. You never want to get into the mindset that a job will be there forever. The goal is to stay focused but remain flexible.

"Dreams are lovely but they are just dreams. Fleeting, ephemeral, pretty. But dreams do not come true just because you dream them. It's hard work that makes things happen. It's hard work that creates change."

- Shonda Rhimes

"Impossible is just a big word thrown around by small men who find it easier to live in the world they've been given than to explore the power they have to change it. Impossible is not a fact. It's an opinion. Impossible is not a declaration. It's a dare. Impossible is potential. Impossible is temporary. Impossible is nothing."

- Muhammad Ali

CONCLUSION

If you have read up to this point, it means that you know you are destined to be great. This also means that you know that the guidance you have been receiving from others up to this point, though beneficial, may not be enough to prepare you for where you are heading in life. This generation was built on the backs of the generations before us. It is up to all of us, that no matter where our loved ones are in life, or the upbringing that we had; that we do better. Don't be content with repeating the same patterns that got them to where they are. Even if your household was successful, you still want to improve, there are still situations or resources that could have been avoided or capitalized on. And for those who are the first in the family, to make it out the mud, out the area where you are from; you owe your family, friends, and loved one's achievements. There are so many sacrifices or decisions that were made, that you weren't even aware of to get you to where you are today. So now that you are here, it is up to you to build and progress. Don't throw away all the work you put in thus far. To get as far as you have gone, just to go right back would be a disservice to not only yourself, but everyone who made sacrifices because they believed in you. Don't get discouraged by the obstacles you will face. Stay resilient, stay focused, and keep fighting. You earned the right to be in any space you are in.

To the young ones just beginning their journey. I applaud you for reading this far. You are passionate, and you know that there is more to life than where you are right now. You are wiser than your years show. More importantly, you are seeking guidance early. As you take these words and you begin to build your blueprint, remember this is your plan. A lot of people can tell you what you should do with your life, but at the end of the day, you have to live with you. So, make sure that you love whatever it is that you are doing. It won't necessarily be fun at times, but the work you put in and the progress that you make;

make sure you are proud of it. Enjoy and respect the process. Every step, every hurdle, every goal you accomplish is contributing to who you ultimately want to become. Be excited about you.

We are all grinding to escape an environment designed to keep us restricted. To get to a place where we are happy with ourselves and the lives we created. It is not always easy, especially when you are the first in your circle to go beyond the space you are currently in. I am not perfect, and I am still striving, but if I have the ability to reach anyone and make sure they are better prepared than I was; then I will consider it a win. And don't stop at just this book; take many perspectives. Each one has something within it that can benefit you. The more you seek, the more you utilize, the more well-rounded you will become. Don't lose sight of why you started and keep grinding.

BS²

LET'S CONNECT

Instagram: @b.s.x2_inc

Website: bsx2inc.com

Email: bsx2inc@gmail.com if you are interested in future events and or workshops

Made in the USA
Middletown, DE
05 October 2023